This book belongs to

....

....

....

ROYAL
BIRTHDAY
BOOK

Princess Elizabeth & Prince Philip on their wedding day in November 1947

ROYAL
BIRTHDAY
BOOK

Collins

This edition published 1983
by Collins Glasgow

First published in 1982 by
Kingfisher Books Limited
Elsley Court
20-22 Great Titchfield Street
London W I P 7 A D

© Kingfisher Books Limited 1982

Design by Hans Schleger and Associates, London

Printed and bound in Great Britain

Introduction

THE ROYAL BIRTHDAY BOOK is a record of over 100 years of Royal birthdays. On the following pages we see the Royal Family in their official roles, but we also see them as parents and children.

As you fill in the birthdays of your family and friends, you will come across Royal birthdays from Queen Victoria to the grandchildren of Her Majesty the Queen. Do your friends share their birthdays? You need never forget another birthday again.

January 1

....

....

....

January 2

....

....

....

January 3

....

....

....

Prince William on his christening day with his
father and mother, the Prince and Princess of Wales

January 4

....

....

....

January 5

....

....

....

January 6

....

....

....

January 7

....

....

....

January 8

....

....

....

January 9

....

....

....

January 10

....

....

....

January 11

....

....

....

January 12

....

....

....

January 13

....

....

....

January 14

....

....

....

January 15

HRH PRINCESS MICHAEL OF KENT 1945

....

....

January 16

....

....

....

January 17

....

....

....

Princess Michael of Kent with her son Lord Frederick Windsor

January 18

....

....

....

January 19

....

....

....

January 20

....

....

....

January 21

....

....

....

January 22

....

....

....

January 23

....

....

....

January 24

....

....

....

January 25

....

....

....

January 26

....

....

....

January 27

....

....

....

January 28

....

....

....

January 29

....

....

....

January 30

....

....

....

January 31

....

....

....

February 1

....

....

....

February 2

....

....

....

February 3

....

....

....

Queen Victoria's dolls

February 4

....

....

....

February 5

....

....

....

February 6

....

....

....

February 7

EARL OF HAREWOOD 1923

....

....

February 8

....

....

....

February 9

....

....

....

Viscount Lascelles later the Earl of Harewood, and his
younger brother Gerald, with their mother the Princess Royal

February 10

....

....

....

February 11

....

....

....

February 12

....

....

....

February 13

....

....

....

February 14

....

....

....

February 15

....

....

....

February 16

....

....

....

February 17

....

....

....

February 18

....

....

....

February 19

HRH PRINCE ANDREW 1960

....

....

February 20

....

....

....

February 21

....

....

....

Prince Andrew on his 21st birthday

February 22

HRH THE DUCHESS OF KENT 1933

....

....

February 23

....

....

....

The Duchess of Kent on her way to St Paul's Cathedral to
celebrate the marriage of Prince Charles & Lady Diana Spencer

February 24

....

....

....

February 25

....

....

....

February 26

....

....

....

February 27

....

....

....

February 28

....

....

....

February 29

JAMES OGILVY 1964

....

....

James Ogilvy

Lady Rose Windsor daughter of the
Duke and Duchess of Gloucester

March 1

LADY ROSE WINDSOR 1980

....

....

March 2

....

....

March 3

....

....

....

March 4

....

....

....

March 5

....

....

....

March 6

....

....

....

March 7

EARL OF SNOWDON 1930

....

....

The Earl of Snowdon

March 8

....

....

....

March 9

....

....

....

March 10

HRH PRINCE EDWARD 1964

....

....

March 11

....

....

....

HRH Prince Edward

March 12

....

....

....

March 13

....

....

....

March 14

....

....

....

March 15

....

....

....

March 16

....

....

March 17

....

....

March 18

....

....

March 19

....

....

....

March 20

....

....

....

March 21

....

....

....

March 22

....

....

....

March 23

....

....

....

March 24

....

....

....

March 25

....

....

....

March 26

....

....

....

March 27

....

....

....

March 28

....

....

....

March 29

....

....

....

March 30

....

....

....

March 31

....

....

....

previous pages Royal Wedding Group *see back for Who's Who*

April 1

....
....
....

April 2

....
....
....

April 3

....
....
....

April 4

....

....

....

April 5

....

....

....

April 6

LORD FREDERICK WINDSOR 1979

....

....

April 7

....

....

....

April 8

....

....

....

April 9

....

....

....

Lord Frederick Windsor & his mother Princess Michael of Kent

April 10

....
....
....

April 11

....
....
....

April 12

....
....
....

April 13

....
....
....

David, Viscount Linley & Lady Sarah Armstrong-Jones
pose for their father, the Earl of Snowdon, in their school uniforms

April 14

....

....

....

April 15

....

....

....

April 16

....

....

....

April 17

....

....

....

April 18

....

....

....

Young ladies putting finishing touches to the cake
celebrating the christening of Princess Elizabeth in 1926.
The cake weighed 150 lb with a silver cradle as a centre with the
baby's initials and coronet, eight cupids holding festoons at
the base and a beautiful chain of national emblems.

April 19

....

....

....

April 20

....

....

....

April 21

HER MAJESTY THE QUEEN 1926

....

....

April 22

....

....

....

Her Majesty the Queen
relaxing at Balmoral in the year of her Silver Wedding

Princess Elizabeth aged 1 rides in an open carriage in 1927

Princess Elizabeth, her baby Princess Anne,
and her sister Princess Margaret at Balmoral in 1951

Four generations. Princess Elizabeth with her son Prince Charles, her father King George VI, and her grandmother Queen Mary

Her Majesty Queen Elizabeth II, newly crowned

April 23

LADY GABRIELLA WINDSOR 1981

....

....

April 24

....

....

....

Lady Gabriella Windsor with her mother Princess Michael of Kent

April 25

HRH THE PRINCESS ROYAL 1897–1965

....

....

April 26

....

....

....

Princess Mary the eldest daughter of King George V

April 27

....

....

....

April 28

LADY HELEN WINDSOR 1964

....

....

April 29

....

....

....

April 30

....

....

....

Lady Helen Windsor photographed by her father the Duke of Kent
on the morning of her confirmation in 1978

MAY

May 1

LADY SARAH ARMSTRONG-JONES 1964

....

....

May 2

....

....

....

May 3

....

....

....

May 4

....

....

....

May 5

....

....

....

Lady Sarah Armstrong-Jones daughter of Princess Margaret

May 6

....

....

....

May 7

....

....

....

May 8

....

....

....

May 9

....

....

....

Queen Elizabeth the Queen Mother as a child at Glamis Castle in 1909

May 10

....

....

....

May 11

....

....

....

May 12

....

....

....

May 13

....

....

....

May *14*

....

....

....

May *15*

ZARA PHILLIPS 1981

....

....

Zara Phillips with her mother Princess Anne

May 16

....

....

....

May 17

....

....

....

May 18

....

....

....

May 19

....

....

....

May 20

....

....

....

May 21

....

....

....

May 22

....

....

....

May 23

....

....

....

May 24

HER MAJESTY QUEEN VICTORIA 1819–1901

....

....

May 25

....

....

....

May 26

HER MAJESTY QUEEN MARY 1867–1953

....

....

May 27

....

....

....

Queen Victoria

Queen Mary shopping in King's Lynn, Norfolk
with her daughter-in-law Queen Elizabeth in 1948

May 28

....

....

....

May 29

....

....

....

May 30

....

....

....

May 31

....

....

....

June 1

....

....

....

June 2

....

....

....

June 3

HIS MAJESTY KING GEORGE V 1865–1936

....

....

King George V & Queen Mary
with their son Prince Albert later King George VI

June 4

....
....
....

June 5

....
....
....

June 6

....
....
....

June 7

....
....
....

June 8

....

....

....

June 9

....

....

....

June 10

HRH THE DUKE OF EDINBURGH 1921

....

....

June 11

....

....

....

Prince Philip aged 7 with his mother
Princess Andrew of Greece

H R H The Duke of Edinburgh

The Duke of Edinburgh & Princess Anne
barbecuing steaks and sausages at Balmoral in 1972

June 12

....
....
....

June 13

....
....
....

June 14

....
....
....

June 15

....
....
....

June 16

....
....
....

June 17

....
....
....

June 18

....
....
....

June 19

DUCHESS OF WINDSOR 1896

....
....

The Duchess of Gloucester with her daughter Lady Rose Windsor

June 20

HRH THE DUCHESS OF GLOUCESTER 1946

....

....

June 21

HRH PRINCE WILLIAM OF WALES 1982

....

....

Prince William with his mother the Princess of Wales

June 22

....

....

....

June 23

HRH THE DUKE OF WINDSOR 1894–1972

....

....

The Duke & Duchess of Windsor
photographed by Sir Cecil Beaton on their wedding day in 1936

June 24

....

....

....

June 25

EARL MOUNTBATTEN OF BURMA 1900–1979

....

....

Earl Mountbatten of Burma

June 26

GEORGE, EARL OF ST ANDREWS 1962

....

....

June 27

....

....

....

Earl of St Andrews, the eldest son of the Duke and Duchess of Kent

June 28

....

....

June 29

....

....

June 30

....

....

....

Their Royal Highnesses The Prince & Princess of Wales

July 1

HRH THE PRINCESS OF WALES 1961

....

....

July 2

....

....

....

July 3

....

....

....

Lady Diana Spencer at Windsor

The Prince & Princess of Wales on their honeymoon at Balmoral

Diana makes her first Welsh tour as the Princess of Wales

July 4

HRH PRINCE MICHAEL OF KENT 1942

....

....

July 5

....

....

....

H R H Prince Michael of Kent

July 6

....

....

....

July 7

....

....

....

July 8

....

....

....

July 9

....

....

....

July 10

....

....

....

July 11

....

....

....

July 12

....

....

....

July 13

....

....

....

July 14

....
....
....

July 15

....
....
....

July 16

....
....
....

July 17

....
....
....

July 18

....

....

....

July 19

....

....

....

July 20

....

....

....

July 21

....

....

....

July 22

....
....
....

July 23

....
....
....

July 24

....

....

....

July 25

....

....

Lord Nicholas Windsor aged 5, surrounded by his family

July 26

....
....
....

July 27

....
....
....

July 28

....
....
....

July 29

....
....
....

July 30

....

....

....

July 31

MARINA OGILVY 1966

....

....

Marina Ogilvy hugging her mother Princess Alexandra

August 1

....

....

....

August 2

....

....

....

August 3

....

....

....

August 4

HER MAJESTY QUEEN ELIZABETH,
THE QUEEN MOTHER 1900

....

....

August 5

....

....

....

August 6

....

....

....

August 7

....

....

....

Queen Elizabeth The Queen Mother
photographed by Norman Parkinson on her 80th birthday

August 8

....

....

....

August 9

....

....

....

August 10

....

....

....

August 11

....

....

....

August 12

....

....

....

August 13

....

....

....

August 14

....

....

....

August 15

HRH PRINCESS ANNE, MRS MARK PHILLIPS 1950

....

....

August 16

....

....

....

August 17

....

....

....

Princess Anne & her mother harnessing her pony Greensleeves in 1955

August 18

....

....

....

August 19

....

....

....

August 20

....

....

....

August 21

HRH PRINCESS MARGARET,
COUNTESS OF SNOWDON 1930

....

....

H R H Princess Margaret

August 22

....

....

....

August 23

....

....

....

August 24

....

....

....

August 25

....

....

....

Prince Edward, Prince Albert & Princess Mary
the three eldest children of George V

August 26

HRH THE DUKE OF GLOUCESTER 1944

HRH PRINCE ALBERT OF SAXE-COBURG
AND GOTHA 1819–1861

....

....

August 27

....

....

August 28

....

....

....

August 29

....

....

....

H R H Prince Albert of Saxe-Coburg and Gotha

H R H The Duke of Gloucester

August 30

August 31

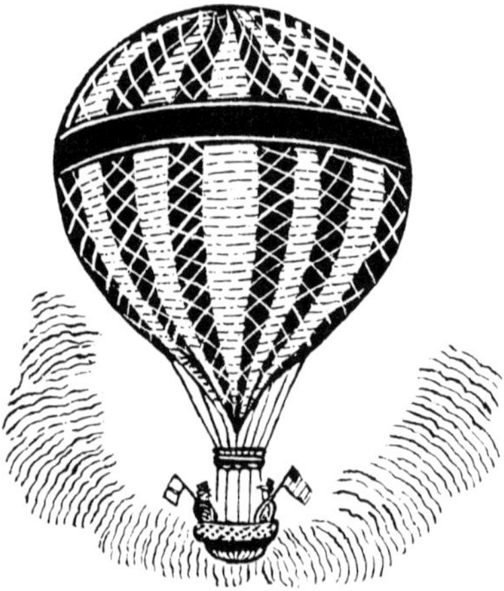

SEPTEMBER

September 1

....

....

....

September 2

....

....

....

September 3

....

....

....

September 4

....

....

....

September 5

....

....

....

September 6

....

....

....

September 7

....

....

....

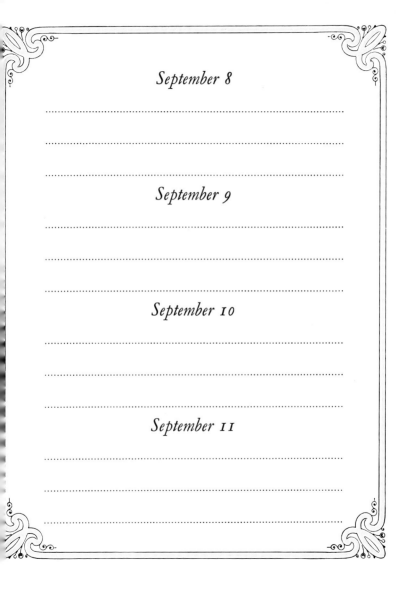

September 8

....

....

....

September 9

....

....

....

September 10

....

....

....

September 11

....

....

....

September 12

....

....

....

September 13

....

....

September 14

THE HON ANGUS OGILVY 1928

....

....

The Hon. Angus Ogilvy

September 15

....

....

....

September 16

....

....

....

September 17

....

....

....

September 18

....

....

....

September 19

....

....

....

September 20

....

....

....

September 21

....

....

....

September 22

CAPTAIN MARK PHILLIPS 1948

....

....

Captain Mark Phillips & his wife relax with their labrador and horses

Captain Mark Phillips & Princess Anne

September 23

....

....

....

September 24

....

....

....

September 25

....

....

....

September 26

....

....

....

September 27

....
....
....

September 28

....
....
....

September 29

....
....
....

September 30

....
....
....

October 1

....

....

....

October 2

....

....

....

October 3

....

....

....

previous pages The doll's house that Queen Mary played with as
a child in Germany. It was made for her by a local carpenter in 1876.

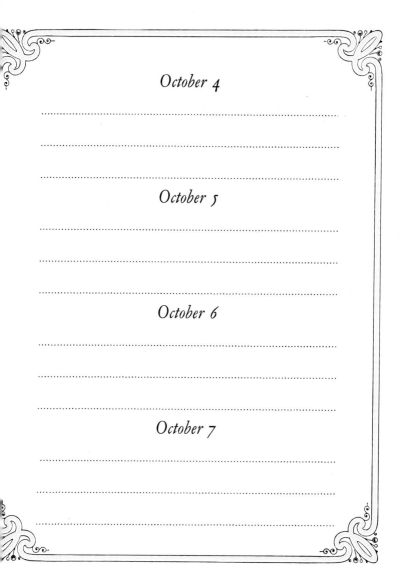

October 4

....

....

....

October 5

....

....

....

October 6

....

....

....

October 7

....

....

....

October 8

....

....

....

October 9

HRH THE DUKE OF KENT 1935

....

....

October 10

....

....

....

October 11

....

....

....

The Duke of Kent enjoys a picnic tea with his two children in 1969

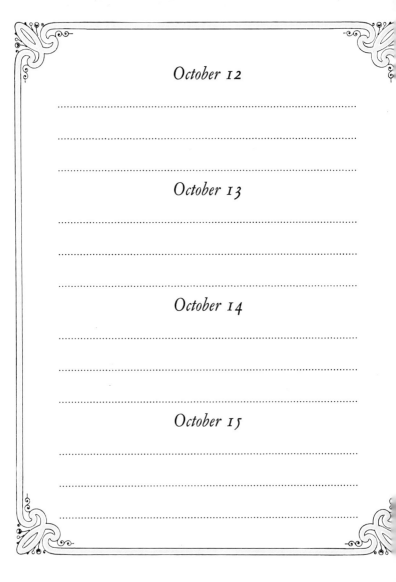

October 12

....
....
....

October 13

....
....
....

October 14

....
....
....

October 15

....
....
....

October 16

....

....

....

October 17

....

....

....

October 18

....

....

....

October 19

....

....

....

October 20

....

....

October 21

....

....

October 22

....

....

October 23

....

....

....

nce Edward & Prince Andrew smile happily from the terrace at Buckingham Palace in 1966

October 24

....

....

October 25

....

....

October 26

....

....

October 27

....

....

October 28

....

....

October 29

....

....

....

October 30

....

....

October 31

....

....

....

Alexander, Earl of Ulster the son of the Duke and Duchess of Gloucester

November *1*

....

....

....

November *2*

....

....

....

November *3*

DAVID, VISCOUNT LINLEY 1961

....

....

November 4

....

....

....

November 5

....

....

....

David, Viscount Linley, son of Princess Margaret

November 6

....

....

....

November 7

....

....

....

November 8

....

....

....

November 9

HIS MAJESTY KING EDWARD VII 1841–1910

....

....

Edward VII as the Prince of Wales

November 10

....

....

....

November 11

....
....

November 12

....
....
....

November 13

....
....

November 14

HRH THE PRINCE OF WALES 1948

....
....

Prince Charles playing polo

Prince Charles with his mother Princess Elizabeth
photographed by Sir Cecil Beaton at Buckingham Palace in 1948

Prince Charles wearing the Balmoral tartan
plays with his cousin Lady Sarah Armstrong-Jones

The Prince & Princess of Wales on their wedding day

November 15

PETER PHILLIPS 1977

....

....

November 16

....

....

November 17

....

....

....

November 18

....

....

....

November *19*

LADY DAVINA WINDSOR 1977

....

....

November *20*

....

....

....

Peter Phillips
with his mother Princess Anne

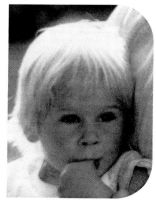

Lady Davina Windsor eldest daughter
of the Duke & Duchess of Gloucester

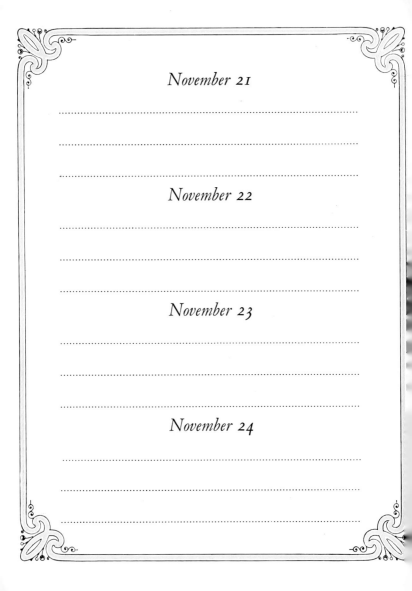

November 21

....

....

....

November 22

....

....

....

November 23

....

....

....

November 24

....

....

....

November 25

....

....

....

November 26

....

....

....

November 27

....

....

....

November 28

....

....

....

November 29

....

....

....

November 30

....

....

....

DECEMBER

December 1

HER MAJESTY QUEEN ALEXANDRA 1844–1925

....

....

December 2

....

....

....

Queen Alexandra with her eldest daughter

December 3

....

....

....

December 4

....

....

....

December 5

....

....

....

December 6

....

....

....

December 7

....

....

....

December 8

....

....

....

December 9

....

....

....

December 10

....

....

....

December 11

....

....

December 12

....

....

December 13

PRINCESS MARINA, DUCHESS OF KENT 1906–1968

....

....

Princess Marina with her son & daughter-in-law
the Duke & Duchess of Kent

Prince Albert later King George VI in his high chair

December 14

HIS MAJESTY KING GEORGE VI 1895–1952

....

....

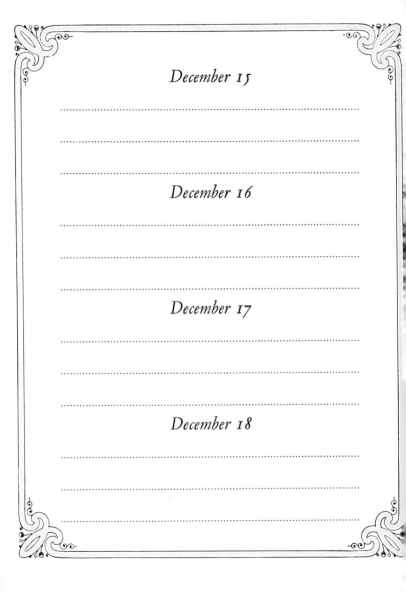

December 15

....

....

....

December 16

....

....

....

December 17

....

....

....

December 18

....

....

....

December 19

....

....

....

December 20

....

....

....

December 21

....

....

....

December 22

....

....

....

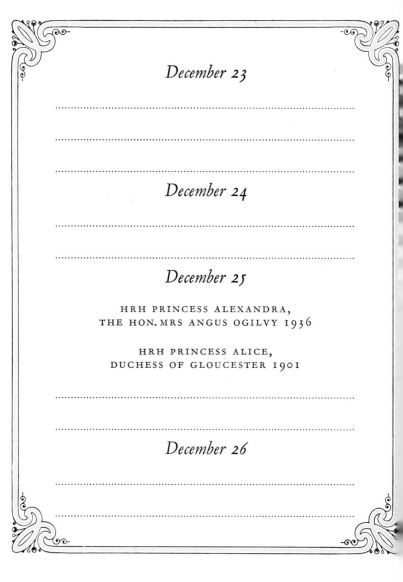

December 23

....

....

....

December 24

....

....

December 25

HRH PRINCESS ALEXANDRA,
THE HON. MRS ANGUS OGILVY 1936

HRH PRINCESS ALICE,
DUCHESS OF GLOUCESTER 1901

....

....

December 26

....

....

H R H Princess Alexandra

Princess Alice Duchess of Gloucester with her family in 1950

December 27

....

....

....

December 28

....

....

....

December 29

....

....

....

December 30

....

....

....

December 31

Victoria
1840–1901

KING EDWARD VII–QUEEN ALEXANDRA of Denmark
1841–1910   1844–1925

Alice
1843–78

Albert Victor
1864–92

KING GEORGE V–QUEEN MARY of Teck
1865–1936   1867–1953

KING EDWARD VIII
1894–1972
– Wallis Simpson
Duchess of Windsor
b 1896

KING GEORGE VI
1895–1952
– Elizabeth Bowes-Lyon
QUEEN ELIZABETH
THE QUEEN MOTHER b 1900

Mary
1897–1965
– Earl of Harewood
1882–1947

George Earl of Harewood
b 1923
3 sons

Gerald
b 1924
1 son

QUEEN ELIZABETH II
b 1926
– Prince Philip
Duke of Edinburgh
b 1921

Princess Margaret
b 1930
– Earl of Snowdon
b 1930

William
1941–72

Richard
Duke of Gloucester
b 1944
– Brigitte van Deurs
Duchess of Gloucester
b 1946

David
Viscount Linley
b 1961

Sarah
b 1964

Alexander
Earl of Ulster
b 1974

Davina
b 1977

Rose
b 1980

Charles
Prince of Wales
b 1948
– Lady Diana Spencer
Princess of Wales
b 1961

Anne
b 1950
– Captain Mark Phillips
b 1948

Andrew
b 1960

Edward
b 1964

William b 1982

Peter b 1977   Zara b 1981

Prince Albert of Saxe-Coburg and Gotha 1819–1861

Alfred	Helena	Louise	Arthur	Leopold	Beatrice
1844–1900	1846–1923	1848–1939	1850–1942	1853–84	1857–1944

Louise	Victoria	Maud	Alexander
1867–1931	1868–1935	1869–1938	b & d 1871

Henry
Duke of Gloucester
1900–74
– Alice Montagu-Douglas-Scott
Princess Alice
Duchess of Gloucester
b 1901

George
Duke of Kent
1902–42
– Princess Marina of Greece
Duchess of Kent
1906–68

John
1905–19

Edward
Duke of Kent
b 1935
– Katharine Worsley
Duchess of Kent
b 1933

Princess Alexandra
b 1936
– Hon. Angus Ogilvy
b 1928

Michael
b 1942
– Marie-Christine
von Reibnitz
Princess Michael of Kent
b 1945

James
b 1964

Marina
b 1966

Frederick
b 1979

Gabriella
b 1981

George
Earl of St Andrews
b 1962

Helen
b 1964

Nicholas
b 1970

Photographs are supplied and reproduced by kind permission of the following:

BBC Radio Times Hulton Picture Library: the Royal christening cake; Princess Elizabeth as a baby; Earl Mountbatten.
Camera Press London: the Queen Mother as a child; Queen Mary and Queen Elizabeth; Queen Victoria; King George V, Queen Mary and Prince Albert; the Duke of Edinburgh; Princess Margaret; Captain Mark Phillips and Princess Anne with their labrador; Prince Edward and Prince Andrew; Prince Charles playing polo. *David Bailey:* Prince Michael of Kent.
Baron: the wedding of Her Majesty the Queen and Prince Philip; Princess Elizabeth, Prince Charles, King George VI and Queen Mary; Princess Alice.
Cecil Beaton: the Duke and Duchess of Windsor; Prince Charles with his mother, Princess Elizabeth. *Charles de la Court:* Lady Rose Windsor.
Tony Drabble: Lady Diana Spencer at Windsor. *Stewart Ferguson:* the Prince and Princess of Wales on honeymoon. *Tim Graham:* Prince Edward.
Tom Hustler: the Duke of Kent with his children. *HRH Duke of Kent:* Lady Helen Windsor. *Barry Lategan:* Earl of St Andrews. *Patrick Lichfield:* James Ogilvy; Royal wedding group; the Queen at Balmoral; Zara Phillips and Princess Anne; the Duke of Edinburgh and Princess Anne; Angus Ogilvy; Prince Charles and Lady Sarah Armstrong-Jones; Peter Phillips and Princess Anne. *Norman Parkinson:* Lord Frederick Windsor with his mother; Lady Gabriella Windsor with her mother; Lady Sarah Armstrong-Jones; the Duchess of Gloucester with Lady Rose Windsor; Lord Nicholas Windsor with family; Marina Ogilvy with Princess Alexandra; the Queen Mother on her 80th birthday; Captain Mark Phillips and Princess Anne; Lady Davina Windsor; Alexander, Earl of Ulster; Princess Alexandra. *James Reid:* Princess Elizabeth, Princess Margaret with the baby Princess Anne; Princess Anne with her pony. *Phil Rudge:* Prince Andrew on his 21st birthday. *Snowdon:* Princess Michael of Kent with Lord Frederick Windsor; David, Viscount Linley and Lady Sarah Armstrong-Jones.
Colour Library International: the Duchess of Kent; the Prince and Princess of Wales kiss.
The Mansell Collection: Earl of Harewood; Princess Mary; Prince Edward, Albert and Princess Mary; Prince Albert; Edward VII; Queen Alexandra.
The Museum of London: Queen Victoria's dolls; Queen Mary's doll's house.
Rex Features: the Earl of Snowdon; the Prince and Princess of Wales on the steps of St Paul's; Lady Diana Spencer on her Welsh tour; David, Viscount Linley; Princess Marina of Kent.
Syndication International: the Coronation of Queen Elizabeth II; HRH Prince William of Wales.

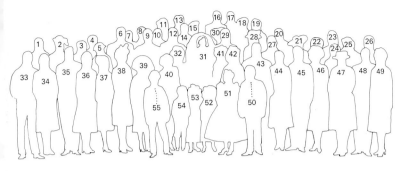

1	The Prince of Denmark
2	Queen Margrethe of Denmark
3	King Olav of Norway
4	James Ogilvy
5	Marina Ogilvy
6	Captain Mark Phillips
7	The Hon. Angus Ogilvy
8	Princess Alexandra
9	Prince Andrew
10	Viscount Linley
11	The Duchess of Gloucester
12	Prince Philip
13	The Duke of Gloucester
14	Prince Edward
15	Princess Alice
16	The Duke of Kent
17	Earl of St Andrews
18	The Duchess of Kent
19	Viscount Althorp
20	Prince Michael of Kent
21	Princess Michael of Kent
22	Princess Grace of Monaco
23	Albert, Hereditary Prince of Monaco
24	Prince Claus of the Netherlands
25	Princess Gina of Liechtenstein
26	Prince Franz Josef of Liechtenstein
27	Robert Fellowes
28	Lady Jane Fellowes
29	The Prince of Wales
30	Ruth, Lady Fermoy
31	The Princess of Wales
32	India Hicks
33	King Carl Gustav of Sweden
34	Queen Silvia of Sweden
35	King Baudouin of Belgium
36	Queen Fabiola of Belgium
37	Princess Margaret
38	Princess Anne
39	The Queen Mother
40	Her Majesty The Queen
41	Lady Sarah Armstrong-Jones
42	The Hon. Mrs Shand Kydd
43	Earl Spencer
44	Lady Sarah McCorquodale
45	Neil McCorquodale
46	Queen Beatrix of the Netherlands
47	Lady Helen Windsor
48	Grand Duke Jean of Luxembourg
49	Grand Duchess of Luxembourg
50	Lord Nicholas Windsor
51	Sarah-Jane Gaselee
52	Clementine Hambro
53	Catherine Cameron
54	Earl of Ulster
55	Edward van Cutsem